ACADEMY OF LEXINGTON
LEXINGTON KENTUCKY
KINDERGARTEN

Let's Look at Rocks
Cipriano, Jeri S.

READING FIRST

Yellow Umbrella Books are published by Capstone Press
151 Good Counsel Drive, P.O. Box 669, Mankato, Minnesota 56002
www.capstonepress.com

Library of Congress Cataloging-in-Publication Data
Cipriano, Jeri S.
    Let's look at rocks / by Jeri Cipriano.
    p. cm.
    Contents: Rocks everywhere—Rocks tell stories—People use rocks—Let's look at
rocks!
    ISBN 0-7368-2938-5 (hardcover)—ISBN 0-7368-2897-4 (softcover)
    1. Rocks—Juvenile literature. [1. Rocks.] I. Title.
QE432.2.C57 2004
552—dc21   2003008411

Editorial Credits

Editorial Director: Mary Lindeen
Editor: Jennifer VanVoorst
Photo Researchers: Scott Thoms, Wanda Winch
Developer: Raindrop Publishing

Photo Credits

Cover: Creatas; Title Page: Royalty-Free/Corbis; Page 2: Mark Andersen/RubberBall
Productions; Page 3: Creatas; Page 4: Royalty-Free/Corbis; Page 5: Andersen-Ross/
Brand X Pictures; Page 6: Chinch Gryniewicz/Ecoscene/Corbis; Page 7: Pat O'Hara/
Corbis; Page 8: DigitalVision; Page 9: S. Alden/PhotoLink/PhotoDisc; Page 10: Jim
Linna/PhotoDisc; Page 11: Tom Bean/Corbis; Page 12: Martial Colomb/PhotoDisc;
Page 13: Tom Owen Edmunds/Corbis; Page 14: Richard T. Nowitz/Corbis; Page 15:
EyeWire; Page 16: Brian Leng/Corbis

1 2 3 4 5 6 09 08 07 06 05 04

Let's Look at Rocks

by Jeri Cipriano

Consultant: Ellen P. Metzger, PhD, Professor, Department of Geology, San José State University

Yellow Umbrella Books

an imprint of Capstone Press
Mankato, Minnesota

Rocks Everywhere

Let's look at rocks!
Rocks are everywhere.
You can see rocks in the park.

You can see rocks in rivers and lakes.

Rocks cover the Earth.
There are big rocks in mountains.

There are tiny rocks on beaches. Feel the sand. Sand is rock, too.

Rocks Tell Stories

Rocks tell us about the Earth.
They show where rivers once ran.

Different colors show Earth's changes over time.

Wind, rain, and ice made
these rocks look the way they do.

8

Heat and cold made these rocks look the way they do.

Some rocks have prints of
plants or animals in them.
These prints are called fossils.

Fossils help us learn when
these plants and animals lived.

People Use Rocks

People use rocks. People build
walls and streets out of rock.
They build houses out of rock, too.

People use rocks to make statues. They use tools to carve figures out of the rock.

People use rocks to make
jewelry. They polish the rocks
to make them shine.

People even use rocks in the classroom! Hard rock made this chalkboard. Soft rock made the chalk.

Let's Look at Rocks

Rocks are all around us.
Let's look at rocks!

Words to Know/Index

Word Count: 186
Early-Intervention Level: 14